Retirement Planning

----- ❧❧❧❧ -----

The Soon-To-Be Senior's Guide to an Enjoyable and Hassle Free Retirement

Table of Contents

Introduction 1

Chapter 1:   Readying to Retire 5

   Housing Options During Retirement 8
   Relocating for Retirement 16
   Budgeting for Retirement 25
   Other General Preparations for Soon-to-
   be-Retirees 32

Chapter 2:   Financial Considerations.....................37

   Understanding Social Security
   Maximization 37
   Understanding Your Pension......................... 45

Chapter 3:   Managing Your Wellness.....................51

Chapter 4:   Are You Ready for Full Time
Retirement? 57

Chapter 5:   Self-Care for Seniors........................... 63

BONUS CHAPTER: Important Resources
for Soon-to-Be Retirees.. 69

Conclusion 73

Introduction

"There is a fountain of youth: it is your mind, your talents, the creativity you bring to your life and the lives of people you love. When you learn to tap this source, you will truly have defeated age."
Sophia Loren

Most everyone dreams of retirement. You spent your adult life working and saving and sometimes even putting off fun, just so you would be prepared for these golden years ahead! You've made it; the end is in sight! Your financial advisor is patting you on the back, telling you to graciously accept that gold watch from your coworkers and live out your retirement dreams! So, why do you feel nervous?

As retirement approaches, many people find themselves with more questions and concerns than they ever thought possible! It is only when this part of your life becomes imminent that you realize there is *so much* more to retirement than your financial health and stability! Of course, the ability to *pay* for your retirement is certainly at the top of the list, but new questions start to arise such as: Am I emotionally ready to retire full time? How will I ensure I keep active? Will my healthcare needs continue to be supported during retirement? Should I stay in my house or move? These concerns, among others, should be met with validation as your retirement approaches. Preparing your *whole life* for retirement is just as important as the focus you have placed on your financial preparations for many years. Your emotional health, physical health, and mental health will all come together to play a role in how well you spend what you'd like to think of as "the best years of your life".

When you contemplate your retirement, do you wonder how you will adjust to this whole new lifestyle? You may need to more strictly follow a monthly financial budget. You may need to find new ways to keep your mind sharp without the daily challenges of your job. You may even find yourself with an all-encompassing concern of "what will I do?" For years, you may have been imagining this time of your life- no project deadlines, no rush hour work traffic, no alarm clocks or restricting neckties. Maybe you've pictured exotic vacations or waking up late or just the feeling of freedom- being able to do whatever you wish, whenever you feel like doing it! However you've envisioned spending your new-found free time, retirement tends to turn out different than most people expected. New challenges, adventures, and even anxieties will present themselves.

Your entire career in the workforce has reinforced the idea that your financial preparations and security are the singular concern when planning and working toward retirement. Retirement advisors, brokers, and financial institutions solely focus on the monetary aspect of preparing to support yourself after you stop working. Even most literature related to the topic of retirement is geared toward investing to provide you with financial security in the later years of your life. Because of this attitude, many people spend *years* diligently putting away money to secure their nest egg, but little time thinking about any other aspect of retirement. A common and *big* mistake of retirement planning is to *only* focus on investing and preparing your finances.

Luckily, you have purchased the ultimate guidebook to walk you through the many *other* aspects of retirement planning that your financial advisor has probably never mentioned. Despite what he (or she) may think, there truly *are* other ingredients necessary to ensure a happy, stable, and satisfactory retirement for today's seniors. Planning is critical to the continuation of a fulfilling life after your work has come to an end. This book will enable you to start on the path to planning your retirement in the next few years. You will begin to understand the importance of social, mental, and emotional health after you formally retire, as well as pertinent information pertaining to retirement tax laws, making the most of your social security, getting your health insurance in order, and living within your new means.

You've done a great job up to this point, and through your savvy financial decisions and dedication have enabled yourself to enjoy the later years of your life free from the pressures and expectations of formal employment. Now, begin to prepare yourself in other areas of your life to ensure the transition into this new and exciting chapter is smooth, successful, and genuinely satisfying. In the United States, one out of every eight people is 65 years of age or older. These men and women are in better health both physically and financially than previous generations of retirees and have a wealth of opportunities and options for maintaining healthy, satisfying lives free from stress. All you must do is prepare!

Chapter 1:

Readying to Retire

Pre-planning tips and strategies for a seamless transition into retirement

"A gold watch is the most appropriate gift for retirement, as its recipients have given up so many of their golden hours in a lifetime of service."
Terri Guillemets

You've come to the point in your career where you're quickly approaching the age at which you have planned to retire. Ideally, you still have somewhere between 2 and 5 years left in the workforce, during which you can begin to transition aspects of your life toward retirement- making the change less abrupt and overwhelming when the date arrives. Satisfaction surveys of those employed in the workforce have shown that an overwhelming majority of employees report dissatisfaction and boredom with their job peaking in their 50's, while many people *wish* to retire before they reach 60. However, a recent survey of over 5,000 workers done by insurance company Willis Towers Watson reports that 46 percent of American's *expect* to be at least 65 before they retire. Why is 65 such a common number when speaking of retirement?

<u>Retirement by the Ages</u>

65: The age of 65 is perceived as ideal and earned the distinction of "most popular" to 24 percent of those surveyed, due in large part to the ability to sign up for Medicare, no longer requiring the coverage provided by an employer. An important sidenote: baby boomers (men and women born after the end of World War II approximately between the years 1946 and 1964) are *not* eligible to receive *full* social security benefits before 66 years of age. So, signing up for social security when retiring at age 65 will reduce their monthly social security income by approximately 7 percent. Workers who were born in the year 1960 or later are required to wait until age 67 to receive full social security benefits, so retiring and enrolling in social security at age 65 would decrease those individual's monthly income by about 13 percent.

70: Seventy is reported as the *second* most popular age to retire according to the study which quotes one-quarter of the workers surveyed as planning to work until they reach this age. Waiting until age 70 will allow these retirees to collect larger social security checks- a 32 percent increase over those retiring at 65. Those born after 1960 would see a 24 percent increase in their social security checks. Despite this fact, many individuals in the workforce are physically not able to delay their retirement until age 70 as health issues tend to force an earlier retirement than anticipated for some people.

Age 66 through 69: 18 percent of those surveyed reported planning to retire between age 66 and 69. This is a logical timeframe, as these individuals would be qualified to collect Medicare as well as full social security benefits, and would be allowed to withdraw retirement income without incurring a penalty, but are not yet required to begin withdrawing from personal retirement accounts.

Age 62 through 64: 11 percent of workers surveyed indicated that they plan to retire sometime between the ages of 62 and 64. These individuals would have the option to collect reduced social security benefits, but they are not yet eligible for Medicare and would be required to provide their own health insurance until they are of age. Some employers will provide health care for their retired employees until they are eligible for Medicare coverage.

Having a specific goal regarding the age you wish to retire will motivate you, as the date draws near, to really begin preparing for this new stage of your life, and to have everything in order before you get there. Having a plan in place and working on the steps to retirement in increments will decrease the stressful emotions that can be associated with the act of retiring and beginning your life free from the constraints of a formal employment.

After you have established the age at which you hope to begin your retirement, the next consideration you'll need to address is your living situation. It's a smart idea to begin thinking about your housing and living needs and options *before* you formally retire, so you are better able to understand and predict your financial needs *during* your retirement. There are several options you'll want to consider when making a decision regarding keeping your home, moving to a new home, apartment, or senior living community.

Housing Options During Retirement

Deciding what to do with the current home you live in can be an overwhelming task wrought with a spectrum of emotions from sadness and fear to excitement. Depending on your current housing situation you may decide to stay in your home, to sell it, or maybe even rent it out, transfer it to a child or family member. You may decide to move into an apartment, a senior living facility for retirees with active lifestyles, or even move in with a child or other member of your family. You are at a point where the opportunities are abundant and you have a multitude of options to explore.

Your choices regarding your living situation will vary, especially if you currently do not own your home. In this case, you won't need to worry about selling a current residence, but you may want to consider what your ultimate plan will be. Will you stay in your current apartment for a set amount of time? Should you plan to end your lease at the end of your contract? Will you rent another apartment, buy a home outright, or move to a retirement community? Weigh all your options and consider their financial as well as emotional and even physical impact. For example, evaluate the terrain of your current apartment building or complex. Is your home easily accessible on the ground floor or through the use of an elevator, or do you need to regularly climb stairs to reach your front door? You may feel comfortable where you are now, but take the time to consider how well your space will meet your needs as you continue to age throughout your retirement years.

Chapter 1: Readying to Retire

Here, we will examine in detail some options pertaining to retirement living in terms of location, selling an existing home, and other important aspects of your housing needs. You will want to consider what your life may look like during these years. Ask yourself if you plan to travel often, perhaps taking exotic vacations or visiting with children and grandchildren often or for extended periods of time. Consider whether you currently have your home mortgage paid off or plan to prior to your retirement. This will most likely be a prominent deciding factor in the ability to stay in your current home, and will financially impact your ability to move to a new location. Many homeowners who are preparing to retire soon elect to downsize their homes, no longer needing the extra space they once required while raising young families. Others could not fathom leaving the home they once shared with their young children and opt to continue living in their homes for as long as good health allows.

Selling Your Home:

Placing your house up for sale can be a great option for some retirees. If you currently own your home outright or if you have accrued a large amount of equity in your home, selling can provide you with a boost to your financial needs for retirement. Keep in mind that as long as you have lived in the home for the last two out of at least five years from the sale of your current home, you can exclude up to $250,000 of the capital gain when you sell your house, and up to $500,000 if you're married. This may be a good option if you feel your finances could use an extra push and if the housing market in your area is healthy.

Selling your home may also be a viable option if your home may be difficult for you to navigate as you age. Stairs, long distances inside the home, as well as from garages and parking spaces to the entrance, may become more than just a nuisance if you require extra assistance.

Additionally, you may be contemplating moving to a different state, or even a different country to retire. In this case, you may be interested in selling your home and renting for a period in the new location before you buy your retirement property, just to make sure it indeed is the perfect place for you to retire.

When making the decision to sell, you'll not only want to consider your ability to continue to pay the mortgage using your retirement income (if you still have a mortgage to be paid) but you'll also want to consider the other expenses that will continue to be required for your home. The older your home is, the more maintenance it will generally require. Similarly, the larger your home is the greater impact it will have on both your finances as well as your time. The cost of your utilities is another financial obligation you'll want to consider. The extra space you once used for your own children may now be infrequently used during holiday gatherings or when a child or grandchild come to visit. Regardless of how often you use these extra rooms, you'll *still* be paying to heat and cool them with the rest of your space, not to mention you'll be paying property taxes on the overall size of your home. Additionally, when you first purchased your home you may have zeroed in on a prime location with amenities that you needed at the time: perhaps the best school district, a great neighborhood, or close to convenient shopping. These perks may no longer be necessities in this stage of your life, but your property tax will still reflect them. Consider if you might benefit in retirement from using those extra funds your large home requires in other areas of your life. Reviewing these benefits that selling can provide can help you decide if it may be an appropriate option for your situation.

Staying in Your Current Home:

When you decide to sell your home, your goal would most likely be to rent or buy a smaller property with cash from the sale of your original home. If your plan is to rent, you'll be paying out money that you'll never get a return on. For some people, it is a better financial decision to stay in their current home, even with the additional expenses, rather than needing to budget for a monthly rental payment.

This option will be dependent upon the equity you have available in your home. If you no longer have a mortgage (or you're about to pay the remaining balance) you'll want to compare the expenses required for your home (average maintenance costs, taxes, association fees, upkeep, etc.) with the expense of either purchasing in cash a downsized home, or renting an apartment. If you find that you have low equity available in your current home, or you are not close to owning the home outright, staying in your home might not be a financially beneficial decision, especially when the cost of taxes, maintenance, and upkeep are factored into your continued monthly mortgage payment.

Staying in your home, even a short while longer, may also be beneficial if the value of your property is appreciating. Depending on your local real estate market, you may want to consider speaking with a real estate agent to understand how you could financially benefit from keeping your home for several years.

There are, of course, reasons that some retirees choose to stay in their homes that are not financially motivated. Some couples may have lived in their home for most of their lives, raising their children and making memories that revolve around their home. The attachment they feel to their home, and the positive emotions associated, may be vitally important to their satisfaction during retirement. This is also an equally valid reason to stay in a home, provided they are financially capable of continuing to live there.

While preparing to retire, there is certainly no one size fits all path for everyone to follow. For this reason, it is important to begin evaluating these aspects of your life beforehand and preparing to make decisions about how to proceed once you have officially retired. If you find yourself faced with a difficult decision, particularly regarding the options of selling vs. staying, it can help to review the positive and negative outcomes of each option relating to your specific situation. Gather your financial information and review your projected monthly income based on your investments and social security checks. Then, list the cost of each option you are considering from selling your home and renting or buying a smaller home to staying in your home and paying the taxes, maintenance, and mortgage if applicable. This information will greatly influence your decision one way or another and will allow you to then focus on the positives of your new situation. Consider the many benefits of downsizing from greater financial freedom to more free time, or celebrate the opportunity to continue the rest of your life surrounded by memories of your children that contribute to your emotional well-being.

Senior Living Options:

Today, there is a vast range of senior-specific living and housing options that cater to a generation of active retirees. Traditionally, most people equate senior living with the term "nursing home", where elderly people are treated as patients and receive care from qualified medically trained employees. While this setting *is* a necessary living arrangement for some retirees, there are other communities that cater to an active aging population who don't require medical (or any) assistance. Known as **active or independent living communities**, these options are designed for healthy seniors, usually over the age of 55, who want to maintain their independent living style while having easy access to helpful amenities like transportation services, social events, and even cleaning and laundry services. Each community has various options as to services available, and you should consider what amenities you might be interested in when contemplating which community might be of interest to you. Some communities have just a few services designed to help keep residents active and social. This may be a retiree-specific neighborhood with a clubhouse, gym, maintenance and landscaping services, and an active social calendar. Other communities may provide more extensive services including meal and dining options, transportation, housekeeping and laundry services, and security. Certainly, there is a community with as many, or as little, on-site benefits to its residents for anyone who might be considering this avenue of retirement living.

Assisted living communities are similar to active communities, but they cater to seniors who both value their independence as well as require some assistance with their daily lives. More options for aid are available to individuals living in these kinds of communities including medical assistance options, personal hygiene assistance, transportation assistance, and medication services. These communities are desirable for seniors and retirees who may have an ongoing health condition or a partner who suffers from one.

Relocating for Retirement

Another consideration you are wise to begin contemplating now is if you want to relocate when you formally retire, and if so, where will you go? You may find yourself now, a few years away from beginning your retirement, dreaming of the freedoms that will be offered to you. Perhaps you've considered that this newfound freedom might allow you to live anywhere you can imagine. A recent survey completed by Bankrate, a consumer financial services company, found that 50 percent of adults between the ages of 50 and 64 would consider moving once they retire. After age 64 the percentage drops to 20 percent. Statistically, most retirees stay put and live out their retirement in the place they've called home for years. But, for others who see retirement as an opportunity to pick up and move, some thoughtful planning should be involved in choosing a final destination.

Some aspects that are vital to consider before choosing a retirement location are various financial considerations, logistical concerns, and general quality of life matters.

One of the first items on your list of pre-relocation research should be the tax laws for the specific state (or even country) that you're considering calling home. You'll want to familiarize yourself with that state's income tax, sales tax, and death tax. It's possible that you could be moving to a state with a higher or lower rate for each of these expenses, and you would want to know how this change will affect your budgeted income. Some states, like Georgia, give an income tax exemption to your social security benefits *as well as* an exemption to many other forms of income during retirement. This makes Georgia very appealing to retirees. In contrast, the state of Vermont does not allow any exemptions on retirement income and is one of 13 states that also taxes your social security benefits. Some states have varying amounts of sales tax, specific tax breaks targeted toward seniors, lower property taxes, and forego estate and inheritance taxes, all of which may be beneficial to a prospective retiree. In general, states that have tax laws appealing to some citizens are commonly making up for this lost income in some other way that could still affect you. For example, in the state of Oregon residents do not pay a sales tax. However, the estate tax that is levied on included assets applies to those estates with a value as low as $1 million dollars, much lower than the government's estate tax applicable bracket which starts at $5.43 million dollars.

While taxes are certainly an important consideration in retirement, it's also important not to let your ultimate decision be swayed *completely* by taxes. Truthfully, if you were making your relocation decision solely based on this criterion, you would be packing for Alaska! No income or sales tax is imposed on the people who live there, and everyone who has resided in the state for one full year receives a dividend check from a reserve partially funded by oil royalties. Recently, those checks have equaled approximately $1,500, but the exact amount can vary each year. Despite these financially appealing perks, Alaska's cost of living is considerably higher than the rest of the nation, due to expensive housing options and increased prices on grocery items, necessary utilities, and health care. While this is admittedly an extreme representation, it highlights how important it is that you consider *all* costs associated with living in a certain area and that you are aware of new or increased expenses that relocating may produce.

Along with taking into account the general cost of living in a new location including home prices, income tax costs, and utility costs, you'll also want to remember to consider the new expense you will incur of travel to see friends or family, or possibly even receive medical treatment. This last point especially is critically important to consider when debating a move. When you choose to relocate during your retirement, you most likely are distancing yourself from most (if not all) of the network of support you built during the years you've lived in your current area. This is most likely a top contributing factor to why most retirees do not leave their general location.

Weather is another variable that may seem rather trivial, but should absolutely be considered in a relocation decision. It's important to familiarize yourself with the climate *year-round* in the area you are considering. As an example, if you've been vacationing in Florida during the winter months you may not be aware of the sweltering summer heat and large mosquitos that plague the warmer months. It would be quite a surprise to relocate to Florida based on your perception of the location during your winter vacations, only to find you are not prepared to cope with the difficulties inherent to the region's summer climate.

Visiting a potential retirement spot during each season, evaluating your access to important matters like health care facilities, volunteer opportunities, social and cultural events, and proximity to loved ones, are all factors that should be included in the decision to relocate.

As a guide, included below is a ranking of the best and worst states to retire, based on a study done by CNBC[1]. They evaluated financial, quality of life, and healthcare aspects and their impact on retirees in the state. If you've been considering a move and are open to all options, this list may help to point you in a smart direction.

---

[1] Dickler, Jessica, and Josephine Bila. "Here Are the Best and Worst States for Retirement". *CNBC*. N.p., 2017. Web. 30 Mar. 2017.

Retirement Planning

Overall Rank	State	Total Score	Affordability Rank	Quality of Life Rank	Health Care Rank
1	Florida	69.22	1	11	24
2	Wyoming	67.81	4	25	19
3	South Dakota	67.06	15	33	2
4	Iowa	66.26	26	6	5
5	Colorado	64.85	27	17	7
6	Idaho	64.12	14	31	16
7	South Carolina	64	7	37	33
8	Nevada	63.64	6	9	42
9	Delaware	63.59	10	40	25
10	Wisconsin	63.34	33	5	4
11	Pennsylvania	63.23	20	4	32
12	Montana	63.08	23	24	13
13	Arizona	63.04	21	16	21

Chapter 1: Readying to Retire

Overall Rank	State	Total Score	Affordability Rank	Quality of Life Rank	Health Care Rank
14	Missouri	61.73	22	18	28
15	Michigan	61.69	28	12	26
16	Washington	61.31	31	20	17
17	Utah	61.25	25	35	18
18	Texas	61.11	3	36	44
19	Virginia	61.08	19	23	31
20	Georgia	60.55	11	32	41
21	Minnesota	60.49	45	2	1
22	Maine	60.41	37	7	14
23	North Carolina	60.27	18	26	37
24	New Hampshire	60.24	35	19	11
25	Ohio	59.59	24	22	36

Retirement Planning

Overall Rank	State	Total Score	Afford- ability Rank	Quality of Life Rank	Health Care Rank
26	Oregon	59.47	30	30	22
27	Kansas	58.83	34	14	23
28	Oklahoma	58.47	12	39	43
29	Tennessee	58.26	5	38	47
30	Nebraska	57.78	40	28	8
31	Illinois	57.15	32	15	38
32	California	56.9	42	8	20
33	Louisiana	56.74	9	43	46
34	Indiana	56.67	29	29	40
35	Massachusetts	56.58	47	3	10
36	Alabama	56.46	2	47	50

Overall Rank	State	Total Score	Affordability Rank	Quality of Life Rank	Health Care Rank
37	Maryland	55.73	39	21	27
38	North Dakota	55.09	43	42	6
39	West Virginia	54.48	13	44	48
40	Mississippi	54.48	8	49	51
41	New York	53.54	46	1	30
42	Arkansas	53.45	17	48	45
43	Kentucky	53.27	16	45	49
44	Vermont	52.79	48	10	12
45	New Mexico	52.61	36	41	39
46	New Jersey	52.55	41	27	35
47	Hawaii	51.85	50	34	3
48	Connecticut	51.34	49	13	15

Retirement Planning

Overall Rank	State	Total Score	Afford-ability Rank	Quality of Life Rank	Health Care Rank
49	District of Columbia	50.96	44	51	9
50	Alaska	50.82	38	50	34
51	Rhode Island	43.84	51	46	29

Budgeting for Retirement

If you're like most people, this section may currently have you feeling less than excited about its message and content. Surprisingly, having a budget in place for retirement can be beneficial to your mental health by reducing stress *and* increasing enjoyment! It can be hard to believe, but creating and following budget guidelines can enable you to spend more money on things you enjoy than you thought possible, while keeping you from one of the worst financial mistakes people make during retirement-spending too much money too quickly. There are so many factors that can influence your financial situation during retirement (Social Security, part-time income, inflation, return on investments, retirement date, taxes, pensions, healthcare spending, etc.) that you have little or no control over, but your calculated and intentional spending is much more in your control! Putting in the effort now to take control of your impending retirement budget will leave you with the ability to make smart decisions regarding the lifestyle you desire to lead in retirement. In doing so, you might discover that by making a few trade-offs or adjustments in your budget you might be able to travel often, retire earlier than you anticipated, or spend more time pursuing your favorite hobbies.

How to Create a Budget for Retirement:

You will begin by compiling necessary information including:

- One year's worth of bank account statements
- One year's worth of credit card statements
- Two most recent pay stubs for you and your spouse
- Approximately 10 different colored highlighters
- Your tax return from last year

You will review these items to understand *where* all your money is currently going, and use the highlighters to create groups of expenses in different categories following these steps:

Step 1: Fixed Expenses

As the beginning step, you'll want to list all your expenses that recur on a routine basis (either monthly, annually, or quarterly). This list should be divided into three subcategories:

- Essential expenses: food, clothes, housing costs, transportation costs, and healthcare

- Non-essential expenses: cable television, gym membership, monthly subscription services, and other extra monthly expenses that are not essential

- Required expenses that are *not* monthly: These usually include items like a home warranty, vehicle registration, insurance premiums, and property taxes that you pay for once per year. You'll want to remember to calculate the monthly cost of these items so you can include them into your monthly budget.

TIP: To account for the fluctuation of spending throughout different months of the year, make a spreadsheet with 12 months across the width of the page. Down the length of the page, list each expense.

For example, if you spend $600 during the holidays for gifts, include "gifts" in the expense line, and write $600 under the month of December (or $300 and $300 in November and December, depending on how you prefer to do your shopping). If it's an electric bill that averages $150 per month, list "electric bill" under the expense category on the left and note $150 across the spreadsheet for each month.

Step 2: Inflating Healthcare Costs

Once you retire you may go from an employer-paid healthcare premium to one that requires you to hand over the cash. If you plan to retire before you reach the age of 65, expect your insurance premium to cost you somewhere near $1,000 per month per person. It's important that you start to shop around now for an estimate of cost so you can correctly factor this expense into your monthly budget. Don't forget to include dental, vision, and hearing associated healthcare costs that are *not* covered under a traditional health insurance plan. You'll need to know approximately what you expect to spend on these items to come up with a realistic figure for the cost of living.

Step 3: Optional Expenses

Include here expenses you *want* to pay for like travel, fun, and entertainment.

Step 4: Lifestyle Considerations

You'll want to examine what kind of changes you might expect to your hobbies and lifestyle (as well as your spouse's). What do you want to spend your time doing during retirement? Is there an expensive hobby you'll take up or continue? If so, you're going to need to be sure to include more money in your budget for those items. In doing this, you may see that there are some lifestyle changes you're open to making in order to funnel more of your money to things you deem more important. For example, if you're set on traveling extensively, you may decide you need to downsize your home to reallocate money from category to another.

Step 5: Fix vs. Flex

1. Add up *all* your expenses

2. Total the fixed expenses separately

3. Divide the fixed expenses into the total expenses

Chapter 1: Readying to Retire

Now you are able to see just how much (or how little) of your income during retirement will be used to pay for fixed expenses. You'll want to consider this number and how it effects with step 4 of your budgeting plan- how you want to spend your time during retirement. Here is where you will need to make some decisions about large monthly expenses (for example, a house or car payment) and how changing them can produce more available funds for things like travel and hobbies.

Generally, if you're hoping to spend more time having fun during your retirement you'll want to find solutions to lowering and eliminating your fixed expenses as much as possible so that you'll have the maximum amount of money in your budget to spend on activities you enjoy.

So, now that you've established your expenses and worked on your budget, what do you do if you notice your expenses seem to be outweighing your income? To prepare for your retirement, it's going to be important that you identify possible changes you might make to your lifestyle *now* that will help you live within your proposed budget once you exit the workforce.

Consider employing a few options that can decrease your monthly expenses before you retire *without* having an impact on your quality of life:

- *Relocate to a lower cost location:* If you currently reside in a housing market where prices have dramatically increased, you may benefit from moving to an area where the market hasn't been as similarly affected. Depending on the area you currently live and where you relocate to, you may be able to drastically reduce your expenses in the categories of insurance, maintenance, property taxes, and other living expenses. If you consider a soon-to-be retiree who has lived in their home for many years and steadily collected equity with the rising market, he may be able to collect $300,000 in profit from the sale of his home. After moving to a lower cost area and investing this profit, he has freed up money within his monthly budget *while* generating income on the interest he earns from the investment. You may be able to simply downsize your current home while still residing in the same area, eliminating extra expenses that may put pressure on your post-retirement budget.

- *Pay off your mortgage:* In order to simplify your cash flow and reduce financial stress during your retirement, you may want to pay off your home in the time you have available to you before you retire (If you haven't done so already.). During this pre-retirement phase of your planning, research the cost benefit of refinancing your mortgage, or simply increase your monthly mortgage payments so that the final payment and the date you retire are the same.

- *Eliminate debt:* Now is the time to pay off the debt you've accumulated and haven't paid back. Debts you continue to carry around are not only draining on your monthly budget, they are costing you money in the form of interest- something you *should* be earning rather than paying at this stage of the retirement planning process.

- *Evaluate expenses:* Take this opportunity to evaluate all your expenses and eliminate any that are unnecessary. As you near retirement you may no longer feel that extra cars or second homes or memberships to certain clubs and professional organizations are as important as they may once have been.

- *Reevaluate your insurance:* You may no longer need items like disability and life insurance, depending on how close to your retirement date you currently are. Eliminating these potentially unnecessary costs at this stage of your life may create more money in a category of your budget that better works for you.

Other General Preparations for Soon-to-be-Retirees

To complete our chapter on general pre-planning and preparing to soon retire, there are a few items you should consider that will aid in a smooth and stress-free transition into retirement.

Estate Planning: You've spent years accumulating your financial portfolio and getting in order everything you'll need to enjoy your retirement. No one likes to consider these morbid possibilities, nonetheless, they can and do occur. If you were to pass away and you do not have your estate properly planned out not only will it cause a headache and heartache for those you've left behind, but they will most likely lose an amount of your assets to things like attorney fees, taxes, and probate fees. It is important that you and your lawyer review your will, trust, estate plan, gifting plan, account titling, power of attorney, and any beneficiary designations. You'll want to have these items updated, ensuring that they are appropriately planned for the stage of life you are currently in.

Documents: To continue the topic of morbidity for a little while longer, your death is absolutely certain, the only question about it is *when?* When that day arrives, someone is going to have to get your affairs in order. It will be *so* beneficial to them if you've already organized the necessary important documents are stored them together in an identified location. You may want to include:

- Listing of all financial accounts complete with account numbers and contact information. You'll include anything on this list that you receive a statement for like loans, life insurance, investments, annuities, etc.

- Wills, power of attorney documents, medical directives, trust documents etc.

- Marriage certificate

- Burial instructions

- Deeds to property, including any vehicle titles

- Military paperwork

- An itemized list of valuables

Be Healthy: You've worked your entire adult life to save enough money to enjoy your time *now*. The last thing you want is to suffer a heart attack or a debilitating disease that limits your ability to enjoy what you've worked hard to create. Making it a point to focus on your health these last few years before retirement can add years of quality life to your retirement.

Prepare Your House: If you've decided to sell your home to relocate or downsize, start *now* decluttering and clearing out your home, as well as doing any repairs that will affect the resale value. You may have been living in your home for 20 years at this point, and you can't expect to empty its contents within a few months prior to the sale.

Check in With Financial Advisors: You might even want to get a second opinion from a fee-only financial advisor to make sure your guy hasn't left any holes in your plans. There are also questions you may want to receive input on from your advisor before making your decisions for retirement including:

- Monthly payments vs. lump sum from pensions
- Take Social Security early, on time, or wait?
- Should you purchase long-term care insurance?
- Medi-gap coverage vs. self-insuring
- What accounts should you begin withdrawing funds and in what order?
- Converting savings to annuity
- How much of your savings are you permitted to withdraw per year?
- How should you organize your assets to benefit your heirs?

Chapter 1: Readying to Retire

You're in the homestretch of your working days, and these next few years provide you with the opportunity to ensure a smooth transition into retirement.

Chapter 2:

Financial Considerations

Maximizing your social security and understanding your pension options

"Retirement: It's nice to get out of the rat race, but you have to learn to get along with less cheese."
Gene Perret

<u>Understanding Social Security Maximization</u>

When you become eligible for Social Security, most people falsely think they should just be able to sign some paperwork and begin collecting what is due to them for their lifetime of paying into the program. In reality, it's *much* more complicated, and this time you have before you are ready to file is the perfect time to start understanding the process so that you are sure you're maximizing the benefits you are due when it comes time to collect.

Chapter 2: Financial Considerations

There are more than 2,700 rules and stipulations that apply to the Social Security program. Even a very diligent person can easily become overwhelmed with so much information, especially when the consequence of making the wrong decision is the potential loss of thousands of dollars. There are strategies to maximizing your Social Security payout based on your marital status, age, earnings while employed, and your needs financially. There are a few general key points of good advice for maximizing your social security benefits.

1. **Waiting**: Anyone can start collecting their benefits beginning at age 62, but it pays to understand that the longer you wait the more money you (and your spouse) will be paid. If you delay collecting until you are 70 you will be paid 76% more than you would have been paid had you begun collecting at 62. For each year that you delay your retirement, you receive what is called a *credit* equal to 8% per year *plus inflation* for each year you defer collecting your benefits past the full retirement age (66 years old for individuals born between 1943 and 1954, and 67 years old for everyone born after 1960.). After you reach 70 years old you stop receiving the deferment credits, so there is no benefit to waiting past 70 to begin collecting.

2. **Know what benefits you are eligible for**: If you are married, widowed, or divorced it is possible that you are also eligible to receive a "spousal" or "survivor" benefit. There are three components to the eligibility requirement for this type of benefit including the length of time you were married, how long you waited to remarry, and when you choose to apply for these benefits.

> *If you're married* you or your spouse are able to collect a full spousal benefit, a payment equal to half of the other partner's retirement benefit.

> *If you're divorced* both you and your ex-partner can collect a spousal benefit amount dependent on the other's retirement benefit, as long as you were married for a period of at least 10 years.

> *If you're widowed* you are eligible to collect a survivor's benefit, which can potentially be the full amount of your deceased spouse's retirement benefits, but depending on when you apply for this benefit the total amount can be reduced.

3. **Only file for one benefit at a time:** If your situation entitles you to receive more than one benefit, for example, a retirement benefit plus a survivor benefit, you will forfeit one of them if you attempt to claim both at the same time. In a situation such as this, you will only be allowed to collect the larger of the two benefits. A better option would be to receive the smaller of the two benefits first and claim the larger one later.

> *For example:* If you're 62 years old and have lost your spouse before they were eligible to claim their own benefits, it would now be possible for you to collect your own retirement benefit plus a survivor benefit. <u>But </u>if you were to attempt to cash in on *both* benefits simultaneously, you would only receive the larger of the two payouts for the rest of your life. So, it would be to your benefit to be aware of the correct strategy for receiving <u>all</u> the benefits you are owed: In this case, you would want to claim your own retirement benefits at age 62 (let's assume $1,800), and file for your survivor benefits once you reach 66 years old (assuming this is your full retirement age). This way, your

survivor benefit will be equal to 100% of your deceased spouse's due payment (let's say $2,469). Now, you're looking at collecting $1,800 per month for a period of 4 years, and then $2,469 per month for the rest of your life. This is a 23% higher payment beginning at age 66 until the day you die.

4. **Filing and suspending:** In order for your spouse to collect a spousal benefit you must already have filed to collect your own benefits. If it's your plan to wait to collect your own benefits until you reach age 70, you can file for your benefits at the age of full retirement and suspend collecting on them until you turn 70. This way, your spouse can claim their benefit without you missing out on the increased payment benefit of waiting until 70.

5. **Divorcing might be in your favor:** As long as you've been married for more than 10 years, both you and your spouse would be eligible to claim your spousal benefit while at the same time deferring the collection of your own retirement benefits to reach the maximum payment allowance at 70 years old. In this instance, being divorced has an

advantage over being married in the sense that a married couple is only eligible to claim one spousal benefit, while a divorced couple can each claim a spousal benefit for themselves. The qualifications to receive both benefits include being divorced for a period of at least two years when you file for your benefits at full retirement age. Your ex-spouse must be at least 62 years old when you file *or* they must qualify to receive disability benefits.

6. **Remarrying may decrease your benefits:** If you're divorced and you remarry before you turn 60 years old, you are no longer entitled to collect your spousal benefits from your ex-spouse's work record for as long as you are remarried. This also applies if your spouse has passed away, and if you remarry before you turn 60 years old you can no longer claim a survivor benefit as long as you remain remarried. If you remarry after age 60 in either of these situations you *will* still be able to collect your spousal or survivor benefits, even while you are married.

7. **Being married does have some perks:** A married person *does* usually fare better than someone who has been forever single when it comes to social security payouts. Being

married for at least 12 months entitles you to a spousal benefit, and you can collect a survivor benefit after being married for at least 9 months before your partner passes away.

8. *For example:* For a married couple to maximize their social security payments, it may benefit them to follow a collection plan such as this: Perhaps your wife retires early on a reduced benefit. When you (her husband) reach your full retirement age (66 or 67), you can file for a spousal benefit based on your wife's benefits. Once you (the husband) reach age 70, you can then begin collecting your own benefits, which will be higher. The effectiveness of this plan will vary, based on which partner earns more money and at what age you each plan on retiring.

❖

Figuring out how exactly to make the most of your social security and ensure you're receiving the largest payout possible can be an overwhelming task. There are many different options regarding when and how to file, and thousands of rules and requirements to the program. These 7 tips are the basic strategies that you *must* be aware of to maximize your benefits, but based on your specific situation there are certainly other variables that can come into play. While understanding and employing these 7 strategies will undoubtedly help to increase your social security earnings, there are also tools available that will account for your specific situation to generate a step by step filing plan to ensure you're receiving <u>all</u> the possible benefits you are due.

"Social Security Solutions" is a software and education company whose goal is to ensure its clients are receiving the maximum amount of money paid out to them from the Social Security program. They charge a fee for their clients, but they take the guesswork out of knowing when and how to properly file for social security. After a consultation with the company, they will compare various scenarios and multiple ways to file for your benefits based on your specific situation. You will then receive an exact plan specifically mapped out for you, instructing you how and when to file for your benefits. If paging through thousands of rules and stipulations before you file to ensure you're not missing out is something you're not convinced is within your realm of capabilities, it may benefit you to seek guidance from a qualified advisor who can generate a plan to fit your needs.

Retirement Planning

Additionally, the government's social security website has an estimation calculator that can give you a general idea of the benefits you might be able to expect, based on the record of your earnings through the Social Security administration. This estimator can provide an approximate calculation, but won't be able to produce your *actual* amount of collectible benefits because it's possible your wages may increase or decrease in the next few years, and once you begin receiving your benefits they will then be adjusted to account for inflation.

<u>Understanding Your Pension</u>

If your retirement benefits from your employer include a pension you'll be faced with the decision of choosing between a lump-sum payment or a monthly payment known as an "annuity".

When you start your retirement, whether you receive a pension payment from an employer will depend on how long you were an employee of the company. Generally, the shorter amount of time you were with a company the smaller your pension check typically amounts to.

Once you reach the age at which you plan to retire, you will need to contact the department in charge of the pension at the company with which the pension is held and apply to begin receiving your benefits.

Chapter 2: Financial Considerations

You technically won't be eligible to claim your pension check until you reach full retirement age, but depending on the specific parameters of your company's pension benefit, you may be able to access early retirement benefits beginning at age 55. Understand though that, like Social Security, the payments you'll receive if you claim your pension benefits before you are of full retirement age will be less than if you would have waited.

Now that you're coming close to retirement another decision you'll need to make is whether to collect your pension as one lump-sum payment or opt to receive monthly payment annuities. The answer to choosing which option is going to be of greater benefit to you is, of course: "it depends."

The majority of individuals do choose to receive their pension payments in monthly installments called a life annuity. This steady stream of income generally helps retirees to feel more financially secure than does a large cash payout, especially if the person is not adept at investing. If you choose to take your pension benefit all at once you have a greater propensity to overspend or spend too quickly, which could leave you short on cash at some point in the future. However, for certain individuals, there *are* advantages of receiving your pension payment all at once.

The first benefit of assuming control of your entire pension at once is that you won't need to be worried about the strength and health of your company. This takes away the risk that you'll lose money if the company goes bankrupt or encounters a dire financial situation. If you had chosen to receive monthly payments and a short time later your company runs out of money and closes its doors, you risk losing any of the money that hasn't yet been dispersed to you. Some companies are protected by the Pension Benefits Guarantee Corporation which can help recover *some* of your benefit earnings in the case of bankruptcy, but there is no guarantee that they will (nor are they required to) recover the full amount that you were promised.

A second benefit to receiving all of the money at once favors individuals who are experienced investors. Once the money is in your control, you can choose how to spend and invest it, rather than leave it up to the pension program run by your company. If you've got the skills needed to manage the money successfully, you could start receiving interest income that may support you for the rest of your life.

Finally, you'll be able to will the money to your heirs if you're in control of the entire pension sum when you pass away. If you've managed the money wisely you could end up with enough money to support yourself for the remainder of your retirement in addition to being left with an amount to pass on to children or grandchildren.

If you do make the decision to take your pension in one large check, it may benefit you to then invest the balance in your *own* annuity. In this case, you would collect your lump-sum payment, roll it into an IRA, and use part of that IRA to purchase what is called an "immediate annuity" from an approved insurance company. Immediate annuities are guaranteed to start providing you with income as soon as you begin the investment. In this way, you've stabilized your stream of income as you would have had you opted to take monthly pension payments, however, you have ultimate control of the entire sum in this scenario. This provides you the benefits of a stable monthly income along with the benefits of assuming responsibility for the entirety of your pension while eliminating the risk that your company could lose your benefit money before they've finished paying it out to you. Another advantage to this plan is that you'll have a stash of money *just in case* an emergency were to occur, or if you would need additional income to keep up with inflation.

When taking a monthly annuity payment from your pension you'll want to consider two options: a single life annuity or a joint and survivor annuity. A single life annuity will provide you with payments for the rest of *your* life. A joint and survivor annuity will pay out for the rest of your life as well as your spouse's. If you opt for a single life annuity your monthly payments will be a larger amount than they will be if you choose a joint survivor annuity because generally the payout period would be stretched over a longer period. Before you make any decisions regarding the payout of your pension, having your company provide you with the expected payout total in both scenarios can help you make your decision. Keep in mind, *if* you feel your retirement savings is lacking in other areas of earnings, it may make more sense for you to take a joint and survivor payout to ensure your spouse will be financially supported after your death.

Always be sure to understand which payout option makes the most sense (and the most money!) for you, because once you decide you won't be able to change it.

Chapter 3:

Managing Your Wellness

Obtaining health insurance to bridge the gap between retirement and Medicare eligibility

W hen considering a retirement date, many people are influenced by the availability of a health insurance option. The cost of health care and private health insurance can impose a financial burden on retirees who haven't reached the age of 65 and don't yet qualify for Medicare. From the point of your planned retirement until you turn 65, you'll need to have a plan in place to address your healthcare and prescription needs. Currently, the Affordable Care Act has put rules in place that regulate a private insurance company's ability to charge inflated premiums to seniors and eliminate their ability to refuse coverage to you based on a condition you already have.

The *best-case scenario* for early retirees is the option to **continue the coverage** you have been receiving through your employer. This benefit is becoming increasingly rare, but some companies and government entities are still offering this option to its early retirees. In this case, you would continue to be covered under the group plan that your employer uses for their active employees, and usually, has a time period attached to it-hopefully with enough leeway for you to turn 65 and qualify for Medicare. Most commonly, your premium for this option would stay the same as it was while you were an employee of the company. Additionally, while it's not federally mandated, most companies will continue a spouse's policy in this manner if it was already included in your premium while you were employed.

A second option that is available is for you to provide your own private coverage through the use of the insurance exchange options that were created in 2010 by the Affordable Care Act. Currently, this market provides coverage for individuals while limiting the insurance company's ability to deny coverage based on conditions present before applying, as well as capping the cost to seniors for plans. You'll be able to sign up at any time throughout the year (not just during open enrollment) because retirement and a loss of existing coverage are qualifying factors. You can sign up beginning 60 days before your retirement date through 60 days after, so you'll want to know if this will be your health insurance solution before you retire.

In most cases, the option that is *least preferable* for bridging the gap between your employment and age 65 is to extend your employer's health care coverage through the **COBRA** program for up to 18 months. You will be responsible for the entire cost of your coverage during this time, and your company is even allowed to impose a 2% fee on top to cover their administrative costs. This is a decidedly expensive and short term option, so if you have longer than 1.5 years from retirement until Medicare eligibility, you'll need to seek another coverage solution.

Currently, individuals who meet specific income requirements can qualify for tax credits to help pay for the cost of insurance premiums. You'll need to work out what you expect your income to be once you formally retire, and if your income meets a certain threshold you may be awarded a credit based on the cost of health coverage in your area. This option can make health insurance more affordable for the period you'll be responsible for your own premiums if you plan to retire before the age of 65. It's important to note that if your employer does offer you a retiree health coverage option you most likely won't be eligible for a tax credit.

❖

Another insurance need you'll want to begin evaluating pre-retirement is your current life insurance policy. For most people, life insurance is a backup plan to provide lost income to a spouse if one of you prematurely passes away. When you retire and there isn't any income to replace, *most* of the time it makes sense to discontinue paying for life insurance. However, before canceling any policy, you might want to review your own specific financial position. There can occasionally be an exception where continuing to pay your life insurance premium after age 60 may benefit you.

Start by analyzing your need for life insurance and the cost of your current policy. It's possible that the cost of your premium may rise after you reach a certain age depending on the stipulations of your coverage. If continuing your life insurance is important to your overall financial plan, you might be able to switch to a cheaper policy while still providing some benefits in the case of your death. In either case, you don't want to cancel your policy without reviewing it and analyzing your overall financial health and retirement plans, because most of the time once you cancel you won't be able to renew at the same rate.

During the time that you are still working (pre-retirement *or* if you continue to earn income after you retire) or if you're currently in debt are scenarios where holding on to your life insurance policy may make sense. If you're still paying off a sizeable credit balance, it would be ideal for you to have a term life policy with enough coverage to pay off these amounts. If you don't have a plan currently but want to ensure your family would be left with enough money to close your debts upon your premature death, you'll want to minimize your premium by obtaining a term policy that will expire when your debt payments are scheduled to conclude, with an amount that is just enough to pay off the debts.

Chapter 4:

Are You Ready for Full Time Retirement?

Considerations for preparing to make the transition out of the workforce

"Half our life is spent trying to find something to do with the time we have rushed through life trying to save."
Will Rogers

Most people spend years dreaming about lofty ideas, trips, projects, or hobbies they will enjoy once they retire. Mainly, most people envision all the fun they always wanted to do but never had time to pursue. Surprisingly, many people in the workforce whose retirement is drawing near find themselves questioning their emotional preparations for retirement.

Chapter 4: Are You Ready for Full Time Retirement?

You've spent years saving and investing in financial preparation so that one day you would be able to relax and enjoy the time you worked so hard to achieve. What most people don't consider is their emotional preparedness-until retirement is effectively staring them in the face! Emotional and mental preparedness is a state of mind, and by spending some time validating your concerns and feelings you can make this part of your transition a little easier.

Start by asking yourself; *"What will I do with my new found free time?"* When you consider the 40-plus hours you spent at work each week, plus any time you used commuting or working from home, you'll begin to really understand how much time you'll have available to you in your retirement years! It will be important for you to find opportunities and hobbies to fill your time and prevent boredom. **Volunteer** and other **charitable opportunities** are a common way many retirees fill some of their free time. Pursuing hobbies like golfing or gardening as well as **traveling** also make their way onto the to-do list of many people enjoying their retirement. Additionally, some seniors choose to take on a **part-time career**, perhaps in a completely different field than their previous employment. This option can keep you busy and learning new skills, and as a bonus provides some extra income! Keep in mind, if you're less than your full retirement age and your income per year is over the maximum earnings limit, your benefits will be rather substantially reduced. If you're less than this age for the full year your benefits will be reduced by $1 for every $2 you earn *over* the allowed limit ($16,920 for 2017). For the year that you will reach full retirement age, you'll be docked $1 for every $3 you earn up to the month in which you turn full retirement age. So, if you were to be working part-time as a retiree in 2017, and you will reach your full retirement age this year, you would be allowed to earn $44,880 in the months *before* your birthday. After your birthday, you can continue to work and earn as much income as you want without having your Social Security check docked.

Another question that many retirees don't consider until it's a reality is *"How do I prepare to spend so much time with my spouse when we're so accustomed to being apart?"* At first, this question may seem unfounded, or you may think it doesn't apply to you. Even if you *love* your spouse, it will certainly be a change in routine to spend most every day in their presence! Most people have a positive experience with this retirement-induced change, but it's certainly something you'll want to consider! Taking up an independent interest or hobby can be beneficial for you *and* your partner.

Chapter 4: Are You Ready for Full Time Retirement?

Many man and women within the workforce feel defined by their careers. This might leave you wondering *"How will I give up my career when I feel it defines a large part of who I am?"* Leaving your career can feel like leaving behind a piece of your identity. It can be difficult for someone accustomed to being partially defined by their job title to transition into a less demanding role. If you feel particularly attached to your position and feel as though it is part of your personal identity, be prepared for an adjustment period where you may have trouble "turning off the switch" on your work to fully enjoy your new relaxing lifestyle. Over time, most retirees find fulfillment and enjoyment in their new, lower stress routine.

Finally, for those retirees who self-identify as a social butterfly, you may worry about what life will be like without the constant daily interaction you were used to at the office. Those of you who consider yourself introverts may feel the opposite about this welcomed change! If you're someone who is particularly fond of social interaction you should consider joining clubs and groups in your area that can provide you with exposure to others with similar interests or who are in a comparable stage of life.

Individuals who have emotionally prepared for retirement by considering and addressing these common questions or concerns will find they are able to intentionally live each day of their retirement feeling satisfied and accomplished.

Chapter 5:

Self-Care for Seniors

Lifestyle changes to start NOW for a healthy and happy retirement

Your best retirement plan for retiring happy and prosperous:
don't be a burden on others.
Ernie Zelinski

Now that you've saved your money, began your pre-retirement planning, and your retirement date is within reach, it's important that you stay proactive about maintaining your overall physical, mental, and financial health and wellness to be able to fully enjoy it!

Your Physical Health

Oftentimes people will point to symptoms that may be a side effect of a treatable medical condition or a prescription drug and associate them instead with the pitfalls of aging. Separating fact from fiction regarding general wellness as you age will help to ensure you continue enjoying your retirement in good spirits and good health.

If you don't already have a fitness plan in place, you'll want to begin ensuring you participate in *some* form of activity each day. Join a gym or take a daily walk in the morning or evening *now* so that when you retire you can continue this part of your daily routine uninterrupted. This will lessen the chance of you not following through with taking up a fitness program after retirement and will add some stability to your daily routine once you no longer have an employment responsibility to get you up in the morning.

Along the lines of a fitness plan, it might be beneficial to begin a vitamin and supplement regimen if you're not in the habit already. Calcium, iron, antioxidants and B vitamins are often beneficial for aging bodies, but always be sure to clear any supplement or vitamin with your doctor before use, because many can interact with prescriptions drugs making them unable to perform efficiently.

Don't chalk up sleep changes to simply "getting older". While it's true as you age you'll generally wake more frequently during the night and require a lengthier falling-to-sleep period, dramatic or sudden sleep disturbances in older individuals can arise from medical issues and reactions to prescription medications.

Be sure to take advantage of the healthcare coverage you have during your pre-retirement phase while you're still employed. Visit your doctors regularly, continue any prescriptions as instructed, and work with your healthcare providers to address any lingering health issues. The healthier you are when you retire the less money you'll have to invest in office visits, copays, and prescription bills. This is especially important if you already know you'll be responsible for providing your own coverage to bridge the gap between your retirement date and your eligibility for Medicare.

Your Mental Health

Equally as important to a fulfilling retirement as physical health, your mental health will absolutely play a role in this next stage of your life. Your own attitude can impact your overall physical health, and studies have even shown that older adults who believe certain health issues are *unavoidable* tend to have more of them than people who don't, specifically decreased memory function and lengthier recovery times from illnesses.

Evaluate and address your overall mental health status and concerns now, because it's possible for these issues to become exacerbated by the lifestyle change retirement will bring about. Following the chapters of this guide can certainly help you to feel prepared as your retirement date draws near, reducing stress, anxiety, and uncertainty that can lead to mental stress.

<u>Your Financial Health</u>

Now, more than ever, you'll want to be sure you protect the hard work and savvy investments you've accrued over your working years. Continue your retirement investing and savings plan up until your date of retirement, and if you haven't, begin living on the budget you've worked up with the help of this guide.

Additionally, financial scams that target elderly and retired individuals are commonplace in the world of today. These scams can seriously damage your retirement if you happen to fall victim to one. Each year, seniors are estimated to lose a total of $3 billion dollars at the hands of financial scam artists.[2] Make sure you're not one of them!

Common scams targeting the elderly population:

Medicare Open-Enrollment Scam: Weeks prior to the open enrollment period for Medicare a scammer will place calls pretending to be from the Centers for Medicare and Medicaid Services. They'll usually state that they're working on issuing new ID cards for Medicare recipients and they need your bank account information and Social Security number to verify your identity. The scammers will then use this information to make withdraws from your bank account. *Remember that Medicare will not call you, e-mail you, visit you in person, or ask for personal information to confirm your identity.*

Pension Scam Targeting Veterans: A scammer will contact veterans over the age of 65 and invite them to attend a free seminar to help them apply for an Aid and Attendance enhanced benefit for vets who are low-income with a disability. These scammers will attempt to convince vets who don't

---

[2] Reports, Consumer. "Avoid These Common and Costly Senior Scams." Consumer Reports. November 22, 2016. Accessed April 01, 2017.
http://www.consumerreports.org/scams-fraud/avoid-common-costly-senior-scams/.

qualify for the enhanced pension benefits due to income restrictions to move their finances around in a way that is beneficial *only* to the scammers themselves. *Only take advice about your qualifications for Veteran's benefits directly from the VA or their list of accredited professionals.*

Stock Market Investment Scams: Scammers will call seniors attempting to sell (usually by intimidation) an under traded stock with the intent of artificially raising the share price. As more seniors unknowingly invest in the worthless stock, the price of shares continues to increase, until the stockbrokers quickly sell off their shares, make a profit, and the value plummets-leaving everyone else with no return on their investment. *Take care to research ANY investment you purchase using an independent source before you buy in.*

Make the most of your pre-retirement years by preparing yourself in every aspect of your life for retirement. Protect your finances as well as your physical and mental health so that you can reduce the stress once this lifestyle transition arrives.

BONUS CHAPTER:

Important Resources for Soon-to-Be Retirees

Locating information for your pre-retirement planning

Below is a list of useful resources that can help you with your pre-retirement preparations.

AARP: This website is a useful guide for retirement and aging. It provides you with information as well as resources for seniors and those planning for retirement. There is even a specific section of the website dedicated to retirement planning that provides information about financial and other considerations of retirement.

The Centers for Medicare and Medicaid Services website has pertinent information about applying and qualifying for your Medicare coverage and will be beneficial for you when planning for your health insurance needs after your employer-sponsored coverage ends.

Families USA is a national organization that is not-for-profit. Their mission is to ensure affordable and high-quality long-term care for everyone. This resource may be a beneficial one to keep in the event of future health changes for you or your spouse.

Helpguide.org is a website dedicated to assisting seniors in finding resources and information regarding mental health, aging, and eldercare.

HMOs4seniors.com aids seniors and retirees in making informed decisions about Medicare options.

The International Council of Active Aging focuses on improving the perception and quality of life for the aging baby boomer generation. They publish a bimonthly magazine as well as a newsletter and update their website which has beneficial information and tools.

LTCinsurance.com is a website that can help you understand and make decisions about long-term care insurance.

Medicare.gov is the official website for Medicare produced by the U.S. Government. There are several links and tools that will connect you with important information regarding prescription drug plans, billing, appeals, choices, services, and enrollment.

The Pension Action Center is a group that advocates for retirees who have problems with the collection of their pension plans. They can help connect you with resources you may need in such a situation.

RetirementJobs.com is a website for individuals over 50 years old who are seeking employment. The site assists seniors in finding work that will complement their lifestyle and skills. You can search their database for positions including work from home opportunities.

Conclusion

After reviewing all the chapters presented in this guide you've hopefully concluded that preparing for retirement entails more than simply socking away money to afford your retirement bills. Ideally, at this point in your life, you still have a few years until you plan to leave your job and fully retire. Using this time wisely to prepare for and map out your transition into retirement will set you up for a smooth and successful transition. The fact that you've considered these pre-planning concerns and read this guide already puts you ahead of many other soon-to-be retirees. Never underestimate or belittle the importance of a well thought out retirement plan and lifestyle transition!

Follow the planning advice laid out in the chapters of this book, and continue to identify any other areas of your life that may need attention before you retire. Having a plan in place will mentally prepare you and provide you with a piece of mind that you haven't overlooked any important factors of retirement. Continue to safeguard your investments

Conclusion

along with staying proactive about your general health. A strong financial plan <u>and</u> a strong body will be fundamental in your ability to fully enjoy your retirement.

Made in the USA
Lexington, KY
01 November 2017